BUT GOD

A COLLECTION OF POETIC WORKS TO ENCOURAGE YOU IN HARD TIMES

CONNIE WILLIAMS WARREN

Copyright(c) 2020 Connie Williams Warren

BUT GOD. All rights reserved. Contents and/or cover may not be reproduced in whole or in part in any form without the expressed consent of the author.

Scriptures marked KJV are taken from the KING JAMES VERSION (KJV): KING JAMES VERSION, public domain.

Scripture quotations marked (NIV) are taken from the Holy Bible, New International Version®, NIV®. Copyright © 1973, 1978, 1984, 2011 by Biblica, Inc.TM Used by permission of Zondervan. All rights reserved worldwide. www.zondervan.com The "NIV" and "New International Version" are trademarks registered in the United States Patent and Trademark Office by Biblica, Inc.TM

All rights reserved. Contents and/or cover may not be reproduced in whole or in part in any form without the expressed consent of the author.

cwilliamswarren@gmail.com

ISBN: 978-1-7329979-8-1

CONTENTS

SPECIAL THANKS 1
DEDICATED TO 2
MY BOYS 3
ROLL CALL AND SPECIAL MENTION 4
TO MY SON-IN-LAW 5
MY FAVORITE QUOTE 6
I CAN'T DO IT ALONE 7
BELIEVING IN WHAT GOD INTENDED, NOT MAN 8
LORD, LIFT ME UP 9
GOD'S MESSENGER 10
CONFU"Z"ED 12
ENOUGH IS ENOUGH 13
CHEATER 14
BUT GOD STILL WILL 15
JUST ANOTHER DAY 17
GOD IS REAL AND HE STILL ANSWERS PRAYER 19
KNOW GOD 20
LET'S CHAT 1 21
JUST SAY NO 22
SHOUT OUT TO SINGLE PARENTS 23

IMAGINE	24
GOD WILL	25
180 DEGREES	26
SIMON SAYS	27
WHAT WILL GOD DO?	28
HONORING	29
JUST ASK VALERIE JACKSON	30
LET'S CHAT 2	31
BEING MYSELF	32
FINDING PEACEFUL STRENGTH	33
IT COULD HAVE BEEN ME	34
SON	36
LET'S CHAT 3	37
CAN YOU HANDLE THE SILENCE?	38
PONDERING	39
KEEP MY EYES ON THE PRIZE	40
AT THE TOP OF THE CHERRY TREE	41
GOD IS...GOD CAN...GOD WILL	43
LET IT GO!!!	44
WORDS OF ENCOURAGEMENT	45
PRAYER OF THANKS	47
MY PRAYER	48
DID YOU THINK I FORGOT TO PRAY FOR YOU?	49
I PRAY FOR...SERVING OUR COUNTRY	50

MOMENT OF SILENCE IN LOVING MEMORY	51
DEEP APOLOGIES	52
REAL TALK FROM THE ELDERLY AND/OR THE SICK	53
MIRROR, MIRROR ON THE WALL	55
WHY HAVE YOU STOPPED PRAYING?	57
WE LEARNED OBEDIENCE THROUGH THE THINGS WE SUFFEREED	58
RECITE THESE	59
DEEP STATEMENTS	60
PRAY WITHOUT CEASING	61
GOD'S PROMISES	62
STANDING ON THE PROMISES	64
MY DESIRE IS…	65
BIBLE VERSES FOR SOME OF YOUR SITUATIONS	66
IF YOU NEED AN ENCOURAGING WORD	67
IN NEED OF PRAYER AND A CHURCH HOME	68
REALTY, LAWNCARE, AND HAULING SERVICES	69
SINCE READING THIS BOOK	70
BUT GOD PUZZLE	71
HOW MANY WORDS CAN YOU MAKE?	73
NOTES	74
SEVEN	75
NEXT	76

SPECIAL THANKS TO MY DAUGHTER.

<u>SPECIAL THANKS:</u> CANICE LASSITER, FOR BEING MY BIGGEST INSPIRATION IN THE WRITING OF THIS BOOK.

DEDICATED TO:

HENRIETTA WILLIAMS
HERBERT WILLIAMS
BERNICE WATSON

MY BOYS

L'GERIK WARREN......MY VOICE OF REASON (JUST SAY NO)
IRVING WARREN JR. ....MY CHECKPOINT
Z'KY WILLIAMS.......MY RIDE OR DIE
LUTHER SMITH......MY OTHER PROTECTOR
Z'KL WILLIAMS.......THE GREAT DEBATOR
ANTOINE DIXON......KEEPING A CHECK ON ME

LOVE AND THANK YOU ALL FOR THE AMAZING PARTS YOU HAVE EACH PLAYED IN MY LIFE. YOU EACH ARE A CALL AWAY IN MY TIME OF NEED AND I THANK YOU ALSO FOR REMINDINING ME THAT ALTHOUGH I AM SAVED, I AM NOT THE SAVIOR.

TROOPER

LOVE TO ALL OF MY BEAUTIFUL SISTERS AND HANDSOME BROTHERS:

ROLL *CALL*

ELDER MARY KING
MINISTER EDWARD HAMPTON
LORETTA FULLER
LARRY WOODHOUSE
PROPHETESS ROBIN BATTLE
ULANDA BRIGHT
PORTA AVILES
MIIISTER JASON WATSON

SPECIAL MENTION

BISHOP JOSEPH & ELDER MARY KING
MINISTER FRANK BATTLE
APOSTLE CLARENCE BLOUNT
PROPHET GROVER JONES
REV. DR. WM MARCUS SMALLS
PASTOR MOSES ASAMOAH
BISHOP BERNARD TANN
MOTHER BERNICE WATSON
TO MY SON-IN-LAW

TO MY SON-IN-LAW
(GEORGE LASSITER)

THANKS FOR BEING SO INSTRUMENTAL IN MY FAMILY'S LIVES AND MY LIFE. I LOVE YOU AND APPRECIATE YOU MORE THAN YOU CAN IMAGINE. THANKS FOR BEING

*MY FAVORITE QUOTE FROM
THE WELL-KNOWN
C. S. LEWIS*

*"You are never too old to set another
goal or to dream a new dream."*

I CAN'T DO IT ALONE

Trying to do everything on my own
And realizing that I can't do it alone
Home, sweet home
Saying to myself that this is something I should have known

Things got really tough for a while
Temporarily caused me to lose my smile
Suddenly I raised my hands up to the heavens
'Cause the devil will not win and send me to a state of depression
Don't need the stress
Just need my mind to rest
So.........I decided to turn things over to God
For He knows all, sees all, and can do all
He has my best interest at heart
Should have done this from the very start

With God all things are possible because I believe
The Word tells me to trust in the Lord with all my heart
And lean not on my own understanding
But in all my ways acknowledge Him
And He '"Will" direct my path

My God......

BELIEVING IN WHAT GOD INTENDED, NOT MAN

How many times have I gone against your will?
Then Your grace, mercy, and unmerited favor prevailed

Sometimes I felt inadequate and then I'd read something and begin thinking
I could have done that thing with a pen and some ink and ingenuity

It seems my greatest enemy is me
Waiting for others to believe in me and my capabilities

This year my mission is to become what God intended
Full of new ideas and things I can share because it's embedded in my heart to care

When you see the changes God makes in me
You'll have hope that since He did it for me for others to see
He'll do it for you too and you can share your testimony

To God be the glory

LORD, LIFT ME UP

Lord, lift me up where I belong
To be what You birthed me to be
To be what You've been training me to become
STRONG
Sharing Your WORD
Being that example that through me "You" will be heard

Even though a lot of times I feel physically under the weather
I don't wait for others to encourage me
I have this gift whereby I can dust myself off, shack myself off, and
Get my mind right, then off I go, after the revision, to fulfill God's vision

You see, spiritually, I've seen who I am to be for quite some time, but yet in my naturalness couldn't fathom that person possibly being me, Connie

Business person, chairperson, spokesperson for the purpose of encouraging others through my testimony despite what others think they see or say, having laid me to rest being judge and jury because those are ignorant to God's process

Having sentenced me to be executed, to die before God's says so....WOW!
When will or will these naysayers ever realize that "I am" "we are" what God says we are... and we are here until God says it's our time

See it, Proclaim it, Be it!!!

GOD CARES

GOD'S MESSENGER

SOMEONE ROBBED ME OF MY FIRST BOOK
THEY PROBABLY THOUGHT THAT TO STOP ME
STEALING MY BOOK WAS ALL IT TOOK
BUT THAT DIDN'T STOP MY THOUGHTS, MY HEART, OR MY EXPRESSION
STEALING MY BOOK WOULDN'T STOP MY PROGRESSION
HOLDING MY THOUHTS IN FEELS LIKE I'M DYING INSIDE
AND GIVING UP ON MY LEGACY
LET ME REMIND YOU THAT IT WOULD TAKE MORE
THAN THAT TO PUT AN END TO ME
I AM GOD'S VOICE TO THE WORLD
I'LL ALWAYS HAVE A STORY TO TELL
EVEN IF I CAN NO LONGER UTTER A SOUND
I STILL WILL BE HEARD BY MY EYES, MY MOVEMENT, AND EVEN MY FROWN
BECAUSE GOD BLESSED ME WITH MESSAGES MEANT TO BE TOLD
SO REGARDLESS OF YOUR INTENT, MY THOUGHTS WILL UNFOLD
SO REMEMBER TO LISTEN WITH YOUR HEART
DIG DIP WITHIN YOURSELF
THAT'S WHERE YOUR HEALING WILL START

GOD'S SERVANT

*AS FOR ME AND MY HOUSE WE
WILL SERVE THE LORD!!*

Joseph 24:15 (KJV)

CONFU"Z"ED

SOMETIMES I GET SO CONFU"Z"ED
GOD, I REALLY NEED GUIDANCE FROM YOU
DESIRING TO BE MORE LIKE YOU IN THE THINGS I DO
SORT OF TWIXED BETWEEN ALL THE UN-ASKED FOR ADVICE I'VE BEEN BROUGHT
KNOWING RIGHT AND WRONG SHOULD NOT TAKE SO MUCH THOUGHT
I'VE BEEN TAUGHT TO CALL YOU UP
THIS HAD BEEN OCCUPYING SO MUCH SPACE IN MY HEAD
SOON I GOT OVERWHELMED AND WOULD WANDER AWAY
WONDER WHAT SPELL I WENT UNDER
LORD ONLY KNOWS WHAT I DID
SEEMS MY MEMORY GOT ERASED
THAT SPAN OF TIME I CONSIDER SUCH A WASTE
FEELS FUNNY NOT KNOWING WHERE I'VE BEEN OR WHAT I'VE BEEN DOING
REALIZING THAT I AM ACCOUNTABLE FOR ALL MY ACTIONS
CONCLUDING THAT IT'S BEST TO CALL ON AND BE LED BY THE
HEAVENLY FATHER ON EVERY OCCASION
NOW I PRAY………

ENOUGH IS ENOUGH

ONCE AGAIN I FEEL LIKE GETTING OUT
NEED A WAY TO ESCAPE
NO DOUBT
I ALWAYS SAY I'M OUT
TRANSLATION
I'VE HAD MORE THAN I CAN BARE
OH, I'M AWARE I DID IT TO MYSELF
I CAN ALMOST SEE MY OUTCOME
IF I DON'T RUN
I DRAIN MYSELF DRY
WHEN THERE IS NOTHING LEFT
I CRY
SOMETIMES I ACT LIKE I CAN'T HEAR
I FEAR
KNOWING INSIDE THIS ISN'T WORTH PUTTING UP WITH
FEELS LIKE DEATH IS NEAR
WISH I C0ULD HAVE WALKED 0UT THE DOOR
I HAVE ASKED MYSELF WHY WAS I BORN
I'M TORN

CHEATER

WHO WANTS A CHEATER?
WOULDN'T EVEN WANT TO MEET 'IM
IF YOU ARE A CHEATER, THEN YOU ARE ALSO A LIAR
AND A THIEF
TREATING A WOMAN LIKE A PIECE OF MEAT
THIS WOMAN TAKES HER RIGHTFUL SEAT

"QUEEN"

BUT GOD STILL WILL

THERE IS A REASON WHY THE "X" IS LABLED THE "X"
HOPEFULLY WE REMAIN FRIENDS AT BEST
AND NOT NESTLE IN A TREE OF MEMORIES WE CARE TO FORGET

TO ME AND OTHERS YOU KEEP BRINGING UP THE OLD
IN GENIUNE CONCERN OLD STORIES ARE TOLD

SOME PEOPLE JUST WANT TO GOSSIP AND KEEP A FIRE BURNING
THEN WITHOUT ALL THE FACTS
WHEELS START TURNING

WHEN I REALLY JUST WANTED YOU TO LISTEN
NOT COMMENT OR MAKE IT A DEBATE
AFTER ALL, MY CHARACTER AND MY LIFE ARE AT STAKE

WHY DO YOU HAVE TO JUDGE ME AND GIVE UNWANTED ADVICE?
YOU WEREN'T KIND OR VERY NICE

I MUST TAKE HEED TO THE SIGNS AND NOT LET YOUR LIES OR MY OVERSIGHT BLIND
THERE IS A WORD FOR ME IN GOD'S WORD, DEAR
IF I ONLY LEND MY EAR
GOD WILL REMOVE MY MOUNTAINS

'TIL MY WATERS OVERFLOW
'CAUSE MY EVERY SITUATION
GOD ALREADY KNOWS

I READ...
HE WILL OPEN SHUT DOORS
EVEN MAKE MY ENEMIES MY FOOTSTOOL

GRANTED YOU'RE STILL MY FRIEND AND YOU'RE COOL
BUT THE HOLY GHOST WILL TAKE ME TO SCHOOL

JUST GET ON YOUR KNEES WITH ME AND PRAY
THERE IS POWER IN PRAYER
I DON'T HAVE TO LOOSE ONE HAIR

THANKS, TALKING TO YOU HAS REMINDED ME THAT
NOT ONLY DOES GOD CARE
BUT GOD WILL ANSWER MY PRAYER

JUST ANOTHER DAY

SITTING AT HOME WAITING FOR MY HOUSING CASE MANAGER
TALKING WITH MYSELF BEFORE HER ARRIVAL AND DISCUSSION OF ME
YOU SEE, I RECEIVED A BIG BLESSING FROM GOD
FURNITURE, DISHES, BEDROOM SET, AND, YES, FLATSCREEN TV

SHE TALKED LIKE I HAD ADDED TOO MUCH TO WHAT WAS DONATED
I WAS EXPECTED TO STAY DOWN ALTHOUGH IT WASN'T ACTUALLY STATED
WHY WOULD ANYONE BE UPSET BECAUSE THE PROGRAM WORKS FOR ME?
I WAS FLABBERGASTED AT THE CONNOTATION THAT THE PROGRAM WAS OVER-RATED

IN SPITE OF ALL OF THIS DONE REDUNDANTLY
I DECIDED TO JUST BE ME ANYWAY
TO BE THE VERY BEST THAT I CAN BE
ISN'T THAT WHY GOD BLESSED ME ABUNDANTLY?
NOT TO APPEAR WEAK AND HOPELESS, BUT TO ENCOURAGE ME

I EMPLOY AGENCIES TO STOP HOLDING THE WELL-INTENTIONED ACHIEVERS BACK

AND PLEASE DON'T REJOICE IN SOMEONE'S LACK
I REFUSE TO LOOK DOWN AND FEED INTO THAT
NEGATISM
AND SHOW MY APPRECIATION FOR WHAT I'VE BEEN
GIVEN

I'M NOT EVEN MAD AT THE SUGGESTED IGNORANCE
GET YOUR MIND RIGHT
DARE TO BE DIFFERENT
BECAUSE NOW YOU'RE BORING ME
REWIND........
REJOICE INSTEAD IN MY VICTORY
PRAYING FOR MY ENEMIES

"GOD" is real

And .....

"HE" answers prayers

KNOW GOD

IF YOU THINK ABOUT WHAT HAPPENED
IT WAS JUST A DIVERSION
SO YOU WOULD NOT FOCUS
AND............YOU BIT

WE ALL KNOW THE DEVIL WILL MAKE THINGS LOOK GOOD
SO THAT CONSUMES OUR THOUGHTS
JUST A MATTER OF TIME
'TIL YOU SAY "DISASTER IS MINE"
AND WE REALIZE THAT WE MUST SEEK THE MASTER

AT FIRST WE BLAME GOD OR OTHERS FOR OUR DILEMMA
WHEN GOD IS PREPARING US FOR A BLESSING
HE IS NEVER MESSY

STOP RUSHING HIM
WONDER HOW HE FEELS
WOW!

LET'S CHAT 1

IT TOOK A BRICK OVER MY HEAD
TO DISCOVER THAT SOMETIMES YOU CAN'T GET
THINGS BACK THE WAY THEY WERE
SOME THINGS ARE JUST PLAIN DEAD

GOD FORGIVES
YOU FORGIVE YOU
BUT YOU HAVE NO SAY SO ON WHAT OTHERS DO

AS SOON AS THERE IS A DISAGREEMENT
THOSE SAME OTHERS REMIND YOU OF EVERY BAD
THING YOU SAY OR DO
YOU HAVE DECIDED TO MOVE ON
BUT THEY GET STUCK ON THE USED TO
THEY CAN'T HAVE AS BRIGHT A FUTURE
'CAUSE THE PAST STILL CUTS THEM LIKE A SUTURE

SOME YOU'LL HAVE TO LET GO OF
OR BE PULLED BACK IN RELIVING YOUR PAST WITH
THEM

PRAY THAT THEY'LL BE ABLE TO FORGIVE SO THAT
THEY CAN BE FORGIVEN
IT'S THERE THAT THEY'LL FIND PEACE THAT PASSES
ALL UNDERSTANDING

JUST SAY NO!!!

JUST SAY NO

THAT'S WHAT I'VE BEEN TOLD

LYING AND TELLING ME THE KIDS ARE HUNGRY
JUST TO GET YOUR WAY IS WAXING OLD

FIRST I SAY YES THEN I START USING MY HEAD

AND... I WISH I'D SAID NO INSTEAD

IF I EVER NEEDED THESE SAME PEOPLE'S HELP
TO MAKE IT THROUGH EVEN ONE NIGHT

THEY WOULDN'T DO WHAT'S RIGHT

BUT I AIM TO PLEASE THE LORD, NOT MAN
AND IT'S ON GOD'S WORD I STAND

WISDOM DICTATES A LEVEL HEAD

SHOUT OUT TO ALL SINGLE PARENTS

SHOUT OUT TO ALL SINGLE PARENTS!
THOSE WHO HAVE BEEN MOMMY AND DADDY, TOO!!!
PRAY FOR:

1._____

2._____

3._____

4._____

5._____

Proverbs 22:6 KJV – Train up a child in the way he should go and when he is old, he will not depart from it.

GOD BLESS!

IMAGINE

WOULD YOU DO THE SAME IF YOU COULD SEE GOD STANDING IN FRONT OF YOU???

YES_____   NO_____

WHAT THINGS DO YOU WANT TO OR NEED TO CHANGE?

_____
_____
_____
_____
_____
_____
_____
_____
_____
_____

GOD WILL...

YOU CAN CALL GOD UP AT ANY TIME AND
HE NOT ONLY WILL PICK YOU UP, HE WILL LISTEN
AND... HE WILL ANSWER YOUR REQUESTS!

I ASKED HIM

_____

_____

_____

HE REPLIED

_____

_____

_____

MY TESTIMONY

_____

_____

_____

BE ANXIOUS FOR NOTHING, BUT IN EVERYTHING BY PRAYER AND SUPPLICATION, WITH THANKSGIVING, LET YOUR REQUESTS BE MADE KNOWN TO GOD

PHIL 4:6

180 DEGREES

DON'T DECIDE WHO I AM BY WHAT YOU SEE
GOD IS MAKING ME AND MOLDING ME
IF YOU SEE ANYTHING BAD, THEN PRAY FOR ME

SIT BACK AND WATCH AS I TRANSITION
FROM A CATERPILLAR INTO A BEAUTIFUL BUTTERFLY
PLEASANT BEFORE ALL EYES

180 DEGREES

SIMON SAYS

SIMON SAYS, "FREEZE"
DON'T YOU JUDGE
LOOK IN THE MIRROR, PLEASE
GIVE YOURSELF A NUDGE
TAKE A PEEK IN YOUR CLOSET
CLEAN UP YOUR OWN BACKYARD
DON'T BE THE POT CALLING THE KETTLE BLACK
THINK OF WHERE YOU'VE BEEN
THINK OF WHERE YOU'RE AT

ARE YOU WITHOUT SIN????

YES_____ OR NO_____

PRAYER FOR FORGIVENESS:
_____
_____
_____
_____
_____

                                                       AMEN

WHAT WILL GOD DO?

OFTENTIMES I PRAYED TO GOD

I PRAYED ABOUT DELIVERENCE FROM MY ADDICTION

HAD BEGUN TO THINK I'D ALWAYS BE AN ADDICT AND UNACCEPTED

DIDN'T SEE AN ANSWER TO MY PRAYER IN MY TIMING

THEN I REMEMBERED...NOT MY TIMING, BUT HIS

NOW I AM DELIVERED

VICTORY IS MINE

HE WILL DO THE SAME FOR YOU, TOO

THAT'S WHAT GOD WILL DO

HONORING MY PARENTS

THANKFUL FOR HERBERT AND HENRIETTA WILLIAMS FOR TAKING CARE OF ME TO THE BEST OF THEIR ABILITY, PROVIDING ME WITH ALL I NEEDED, AND FOR CHOOSING ME!

THANKFUL FOR MY BEAUTIFUL AND LOVING SUPER MOM, BERNICE O. WATSON. THANK YOU FOR YOUR MANY SACRIFICES AND YOUR UNCONDITIONAL LOVE!

****

"MANY WOMEN DO NOBLE THINGS, BUT YOU SURPASS THEM ALL." CHARM IS DECEPTIVE, BEAUTY IS FLEETING; BUT A WOMAN WHO FEARS THE LORD IS TO BE PRAISED."

PROVERBS 31:29-30 NIV

FATHERS ARE COMMISSIONED TO HAVE AN ACTIVE ROLE IN RAISING THEIR YOUNG. LEADING THEM IN DISCIPLINE AND INSTRUCTION TOO AS THE LEADER OF THE HOME WITH GODLY LOVE.

Ref: EPHESIANS 6:1-4

****

HINDSIGHT: WHAT THINGS ARE YOU THANKFUL FOR NOW, IN YOUR PARENTS, THAT YOU DIDN'T LIKE OR UNDERSTAND IN YOUR YOUTH?

LIST ON THE BACK>>>

JUST ASK VALERIE JACKSON

DON'T GIVE UP NOW!

I DECREE AND DECLARE THAT:

_____

_____

_____

_____

_____

_____

_____

_____

_____

_____

_____

_____

HALLELUJAH!!!   HOSANNA!!!!

AMEN AND AMEN

LET'S CHAT 2

WHAT DO YOU WANT TO TALK ABOUT? "HE'S"' LISTENING!

_____
_____
_____
_____
_____
_____

WHAT DID YOU LEARN?

_____
_____
_____
_____
_____
_____
_____

GLORY HALLELUJAH! AMEN.

BEING MYSELF

WHY SHOULD I CHANGE ME

TO BE WHAT YOU WANT ME TO BE

WHY CAN'T I SIMPLY JUST BE ME?

KEEPING MY VISION AND PLAN

SEE NO NEED TO CHANGE FOR ANY MAN

DEFINITELY HAVE NO PROBLEM LIVING ALONE

THAT MAKES FOR ME A HAPPY HOME

STOP TRYING TO CONVINCE ME OF YOUR IDEAS

I'VE HAD MY OWN FOR MANY YEARS

I'M JUST LEARNNING TO BE TRUE TO SELF

REALLY DON'T HAVE TIME FOR NEGATISM FROM ANYONE ELSE

PLEASE DON'T BE OFFENDED BY MY NEW WAYS

BEEN HASHING OVER THIS FOR DAYS

HAVE MUCH LOVE FOR YOU, FAM

I DECIDED TO BE WHO I AM............

I LOVE ME

PEACE

FINDING MY PEACE

I'VE PAID CLOSE ATTENTION AND HAVE THE ROUTINE DOWN TO THE LETTER

ANXIOUSLY AWAITING MY FEELING BETTER

SEEMINGLY GROWING WEAKER, WEAKER, AND MORE TIRED, WONDERING IF ANYONE FEELS THE SAME WAY I DO OR IF IT'S ONLY ME

SOME FOLKS THINK I JUST WANT ATTENTION OR THEY OFFER UP A SOLUTION TO SOMETHING THEY'VE NEVER EXPERIENCED, BUT READ UP OR SOMEONE MADE MENTION

CAUSING (IF I LET THEM) A LOT OF STRESS AND TENSION

HAD A DEEP BREATH AND EXHALE

KNOW THAT GOD GAVE ME ALL THE TOOLS I NEED TO SUCCEED

I CAN DO ALL THINGS THROUGH CHRIST WHICH STRENGHENS ME.

PHILIPPIANS 4:13

IT COULD HAVE BEEN ME!

WHAT A BAD FEELING IT IS TO BE CAUGHT UP!
TO FEEL TRAPPED
CAN'T SEE YOUR WAY OUT
OVERTAKEN BY DOUBT
WHATEVER YOUR ADDICTION
WHETHER ACOHOL, CIGARETTES, DRUGS, OR MAYBE
FOOD
IT CAN RUIN YOUR MOOD
WITHOUT YOUR DRUG OF CHOICE
THE WORLD SEEMS DIM
YOU FEEL TIRED, WEAK, AND IN PAIN
DRAINED AS YOU MAY BE, YOU'LL GATHER UP SOME
STRENGTH FROM SOMEWHERE
WALK CLEAN ACROSS THE GLOBE TO GET SOME MORE
CHASING THAT FIRST FEELING THAT ONLY LASTS A
MINUTE OR SO

THIS BECOMES YOUR DAILY ROUTINE
DAY IN AND DAY OUT

NO SUCH THING AS FUN ANYMORE
ONLY RUNNING IN AND OUT THE DOOR

EYES BLINDED AND CLOUDY TOUGHTS
ALWAYS FEELING LIKE A VICTIM OF SORTS
NEVER LOOKING ANYONE IN THE EYE TO REMAIN
HIDDEN

THINKING YOU'LL NEVER BE REALLY SEEN
ARE YOU KIDDING?

AS I WATCH THIS MOTION PICTURE
I SEE THOSE I SMOKED WITH AND/OR SOLD TO HAVING
STROKES, HEART ATTACKS, KILLING, OR BEING KILLED
BY THIS DISEASE
WOW! IT COULD HAVE BEEN ME

THANK GOD I'M SOBER

SON

SON, WHAT HAPPENED TO THE MOMENTS?

THE ONES "WE" USED TO HAVE WHEN WE FELT THE NEED TO COMPOSE

WHERE DID IT ALL GO?

GOD BLESSED BOTH OF US WITH THAT TALENT IN OUR OWN WAY

WHY DID YOU LET IT GO TO WASTE?

I'M NOT TALKING ABOUT DIPPING AND DABBING

I'M TALKING ABOUT THAT LOOK YOU HAD THAT MADE YOU TICK-TOCK AT BEING YOU

WE NEED TO CREATE

THAT'S THE WAY WE COMMUNICATE

IT'S NOT TO LATE

I PRAY

LORD, STIR UP THE PASSION WITHIN US AGAIN

BRING IT, BABY

LET'S CHAT 3

HAVE YOU EVER TOLD YOUR KIDS
THAT SOMETHING THEY DO GETS ON YOUR LAST NERVE?
YOU COMPLAIN AND COMPLAIN
JUST TO BE TOLD
THAT YOU ACT EXACTLY THE SAME

WOW
WITH LITTLE THOUGHT YOU REALIZE THAT THEY'RE RIGHT
LOOKING THROUGH THE MIRROR OF YOUR MIND
YOU SEE YOU IN THEM
NOW YOU NEED TO REPENT
ASK FOR FORGIVENESS FOR EVEN FEELING BENT

THE COMMON DENOMINATOR IN ALL THESE CHATS IS.......

PRAYER AND PRAISE

CAN YOU HANDLE THE SILENCE?

CAN YOU HANDLE THE SILENCE?
SILENCE WILL GIVE YOUR LIFE PEACE
STOP LISTENING TO OTHERS' LOUD VOICES
TO BEGIN MAKING BETTER CHOICES
HAVING DAILY COMMUNION WITH HIM
FOR HE IS YOUR TRUE FRIEND
MATTERS WHERE WE ARE AND GOING MORE THAN WHERE WE'VE BEEN

LOOKING THROUGH, FOR EXAMPLE, YOUR KIDS' EYES
IT'S NOT SO IMPORTANT WHO'S RIGHT
THE MIROR OF YOUR MIND SHINES WITH IMAGES OF YOU IN THEM, IN YOUR SIGHT
SO LET'S STOP LETTING OUR MINDS ROAM
LET'S PRAY THAT EVERYTHING WILL BE ALRIGHT
SPEND MORE TIME WITH GOD ALONE
LISTENING, REPENTING, AND FORGIVING
MAKING OUR HOME HIS NOME

CAN'T YOU HEAR EVEN IN THIS SILENCE?
REVELATION KNOWLEDGE

COMMON DENOMINATOR: PRAYER AND PRAISE

PONDERING...

People say a lot of things and are quick to say I love you because they think that is what you want to hear!
Manipulating and baiting you in when they don't even like you. They are just trying to find an opportunity to use you. Watch out and test people to see if they are one of the snakes in the grass!

KEEP MY EYES ON THE PRIZE

MUST BE CAREFUL OF LETTING PEOPLE IN

ESPECIALLY SINCE I KNOW WHERE I'VE BEEN

EVEN SO I'M STILL GUILTY OF COMPROMISING MY GOALS AND FORGETTING MY VISION

'CAUSE I MADE SOME FEEL-GOOD DECISIONS

I SINNED

THANK GOD FOR MY MORNING DEVOTIONS

WHERE I'M REMINDED...

THAT I CAN ONLY FIND PEACE IN GOD'S LOVE

NOT IN A THING OR EVEN A MAN, BUT UP ABOVE

NOW IN PRAYER AND ON BENDED KNEE

MY BAD DECISION

I BEGGED HIM TO PEACEFULLY TAKE AWAY FROM ME

I COULD HAVE AVOIDED THIS DISASTER IF I HAD ONLY KEPT MY EYES ON THE MASTER

Colossians 3:2 "Set your affection on things above, not on things on the earth."

AT THE TOP OF THE CHERRY TREE

HAVING TO STRETCH AND REALLY REACH FOR MY DREAM
SOMETHING THAT SEEMS TOO HIGH TO ACHIEVE

AT THE TOP OF THAT CHERRY TREE IS WHERE I LEARN
PREPARING ME FOR "IT'S ONLY A TEST"
WHY DO I FIGHT SO HARD FOR AN "US"?
WHEN CLEARLY THERE IS A LACK OF TRUST

FOR SOMETHING I WAS ONLY MEANT TO LEARN FROM BUT
IS EQUALLED TO MERE DUST
AND NEVER WAS MEANT TO LAST UNTIL ETERNITY

REACHING HIGH FOR THE SWEETISH CHERRY AT THE TOP OF THAT CHERRY TREE
IGNORING ALL THE SCRATCHES, BRUISES, AND STRESS TO BECOME MY BEST

NOW I AM READY TO GROW
READY FOR ANOTHER LEVEL
'CAUSE ONCE AGAIN IV'E DEFEATED THAT DEVIL, YOU KNOW

SMILING, BITING INTO THAT CHERRY I WORKED
FOR AT THE TOP OF THAT CHERRY TREE AND
EXPERIENCING THE SWEET TASTE OF WHAT GOD
HAD WAITING FOR ME
SO I COULD RECIEVE THAT BLESSING I COULD NOT
SEE

THANK GOD FOR THE GROWING PAINS
MY LIFE FOR MY BETTERMENT WILL NEVER BE THE
SAME

WOW! RESTING FOR A MOMENT AT THE TOP OF THE
CHERRY TREE

THE BOTTOM I'LL NEVER MISS
THIS LIFE WITH GOD AT THE REINS IS PURE BLISS

MY UTOPIA

THANK YOU, GOD, FOR
ANOTHER LESSON LEARNED

GOD IS

***

GOD CAN

***

GOD WILL

LET IT GO!!!

A few good memories
But why agonize over them?
In the mist of all the hurt, disloyalty and lies
Why such a bond?
Why such ties?

Why is it so hard to say goodbye?
Why live a lie?
Being mentally abused and beat
When you know the label is cheat
Almost killed you but still you stay
There IS a better way

Think of what you are implying
You're not married, so why keep trying?
Re-think what you are doing
Don't you know by now deceit is brewing?

Why not try God for He is that better way?
Turn to Him today
Let go and let God
Let it go!!!

Trust Him...

WORDS OF ENCOURAGEMENT

"START WHERE YOU ARE. USE WHAT YOU HAVE. DO WHAT YOU CAN."
ARTHUR ASH

"WHEN ONE DOOR CLOSES, ANOTHER DOOR OPENS; BUT WE SO OFTEN LOOK SO LONG AND SO REGRETFULLY AT THE CLOSED DOOR THAT WE DO NOT SEE THE ONES THAT OPEN FOR US."
ALEXANDER GRAHAM BELL

"LIFE IS A SUCCESSION OF LESSONS WHICH MUST BE LIVED TO BE UNDERSTOOD."
HELEN KELLER

"YOU MUST DO THE THINGS YOU THINK YOU CAN NOT DO."
ELEANOR ROOSEVELT

"IT YOU DON'T PAY APPROPIATE ATTENTION TO WHAT HAS YOUR ATTENTION, IT WILL TAKE MORE ATTENTION THAN IT DESERVES."
DAVID ALLEN

"CHARATER CANNOT BE DEVELOPED IN EASE AND QUIET. ONLY THROUGH EXPERIENCE OF TRIAL AND SUFFERING CAN THE SOUL BE STRENGTHENED, AMBITION INSPIRED, AND SUCCESS ACHIEVED."
HELEN KELLER

"IT IS BY GOING INTO THE ABYSS THAT WE RECOVER THE TREASURES OF LIFE. WHERE YOU STUMBLE THERE LIES YOUR TREASURE."

JOSEPH CAMPBELL

"IF WE WANT TO DIRECT OUR LIVES, WE MUST TAKE CONTROL OF OUR CONSISTANT ACTIONS. IT IS NOT WHAT WE DO ONCE IN A WHILE THAT SHAPES OUR LIVES, BUT WHAT YOU DO CONSISTENTLY."

TONY ROBBONS

"OUR GREATEST WEAKNESS LIES IN GIVING UP. THE MOST CERTAIN WAY TO SUCCEED IS ALWAYS TO TRY ONE MORE TIME."

THOMAS A. EDISON

"EVEN IF YOU FALL ON YOUR FACE, YOU'RE STILL MOVING FORWARD."

VICTOR KIAM

PRAYER OF THANKS

THANK YOU "OH, GOD" FOR GENTLY TEACHING ME
THIS NEW LESSON

SHOULD HAVE LISTENED TO MY OWN SPOKEN AND
WRITTEN WORDS

TO MY ADVICE

SHOULD HAVE LISTENED TO YOUR VOICE

THANKS FOR A CHOICE

LESSON LEARNED ONCE AGAIN

THANKS FOR CHOOSING ME

I CHOOSE YOU

MY PRAYER

GOD, I ASK THAT YOU LEAD ME AND GUIDE ME INTO A LIFE OF HONESTY AND INTEGRITY. I ACKNOWLEDGE THAT I HAVE SINNED AND COME SHORT OF YOUR GLORY. LORD, YOU KNOW THAT I HAVE MADE PLENTY OF MISTAKES; FOR THESE MOMENTS, LORD, I REPENT. PLEASE FORGIVE ME AND I FORGIVE. I WANT TO BE PLEASING IN YOUR SIGHT SO THAT IN ME YOU CAN SAY I AM WELL PLEASED. I PRAY THAT THIS BOOK GLORIFIES YOU, IN JESUS' NAME. AMEN AND AMEN.

DID YOU THINK I FORGOT TO PRAY FOR YOU?

++++++++

I PRAY FOR ALL WHO HAVE READ THIS GOD-INSPIRED BOOK. MAY YOU HAVE

KNOWLEDGE OF HIS WILL THROUGH ALL SPIRITUAL WISDOM AND UNDERSTANDING.

REF: COLOSSIANS 1:9

I PRAY ALSO THAT THE EYES OF YOUR HEARTS MAY BE ENLIGHTENED IN ORDER FOR YOU TO KNOW THE HOPE TO WHICH HE HAS CALLED YOU, THE RICHES OF HIS GLORIOUS INHERITANCE.

REF: EPHESIANS 1:18

I PRAY FOR AND THANK THOSE WHO ARE SERVING/HAVE SERVED OUR COUNTRY:

<u>FAMILY</u> (JUST TO NAME A FEW)

HERBERT H. WILLIAMS
   ERSKIN HENRY
ERNEST HARRISON
ANTHONY AVILES JR./SR.
EDWARD HAMPTON
TREVON MORRIS
ZKL S. WILLIAMS
BISHOP JOSEPH KING
AND MORE.....

OTHERS:

_____

_____

_____

_____

*****YOU ARE ALL APPRECIATED*****

IN LOVING MEMORY.............
MOMENT OF SILENCE

<u>NAME</u>   <u>BIRTH</u>   <u>DEATH</u>

YOU ARE LOVED AND MISSED!

MY APOLOGIES

MY APOLOGIES TO ALL FOR ANYTHING I'VE WRITTEN OR SAID THAT YOU FIND OFFENSIVE. FORGIVE ME IF I DIDN'T MENTION BY OVERSIGHT! NOTIFY ME AND I WILL BE SURE TO MENTION YOU IN MY NEXT BOOK.

THANKS FOR YOUR:

LOVE

PATIENCE

PRAYERS

FORGIVENESS

HOPEFULLY, YOU CAN SEE THAT YOUR ENDURANCE WHILE GOD WORKS ON ME IS NOT IN VAIN! DON'T STOP PRAYING...

REAL TALK FROM THE ELDERLY AND/OR THE SICK

Young people don't or won't understand what "we" the elderly and/or sick go through
Understandably so, because it's a life they've never experienced
But if they live long enough, like it or not, they will come to know

When we rise up in the morning, we have to decide what's most important for the day
Plan what and how much we can do, and in some cases what we can say

Enduring all the unwanted advice
Smiling and making nice
For fear of being put in a home
Or being left alone

We hold light to our faith
Praying every day, all day
Interceding for our families
That they will have a long life and one day be able to say
"I understand what the sick and the elderly go through
'Cause that is me today"

Show respect, listen, and have patience when dealing with parents and grandparents since it was them who carried you so you could make it to this day to say...

Young people don't or won't understand what "we" the elderly and/or the sick go through
Understandably so, because it's a life they've never experienced
But if they live long enough, they will come to know OUR LIVES MATTER!!!

MIRROR, MIRROR ON THE WALL

Seems some lack the ability to see themselves and try not to hear what anyone else has to say so they won't feel forced to lock into the mirror of their evil ways

I was just sitting here thinking about the many times I was accused by fake family and fake friends who had been lurking around, waiting for the opportunity to bring me down
You and others sent false accusations my way and were posted with a smile and a smirk, ready and determined to run me through the dirt
Even threw in some extra lies so the story would be juicy and others would be more willing to spread rumors in the hopes that my judgment would be cruel and swift
After all, you had been waiting ever so patiently for my demise

You had the nerve to look me straight in the eye, thinking it would convince me that you were on my side
Lies, lies, and more lies
You even had the nerve to say you cared and would be there for me when it was quite the opposite
Your presence was to hear my sentence and hear my cries

Misery loves company
How many times, how many people did you recruit, convincing them to hate me just like you do?

For no good reason, from lies believed, from a mistake, from deceit

Did you forget you have a date with God? JUDGMENT DAY!!!

What will be your excuse?
What will be your fate?

Matthew 7:2 KJV, I might add, reads:
For with what judgment ye judge ye SHALL be judged,
and with what measure ye mete it SHALL be measured to you again

So when that time comes, don't you dare try to explain
Remember how you and you cohorts cast me out and didn't give me a chance to open my mouth or even ask me to explain

It's a sad thing when you lie so much that you start to believe your own lies and it doesn't even occur to you to repent or to look in the mirror for fear your eyes will tell your truth

Then when your co-partners in crime realized that your crocodile tears where really tears of joy, they blackballed you just like you did me

See, you thought you could ruin me but you did me a favor
You brewed in me the desire to trust God even the more…

Doesn't feel so good when the shoe is tight on your foot
Does the realization set in that you'd better retract your lies before it's too late?
You'd better repent or to hell you might be sent
You fought a focused fight but yet I live
And I can honestly look you in the eye and say I LOVE YOU in spite of…
Now I pray: Mirror, mirror on the wall kill the evil spirit that lurks within, AMEN

God = Love

WHY HAVE YOU STOPPED PRAYING?

1. _____
2. _____
3. _____
4. _____
5. _____

WOULD YOU SAY ANY OF THOSE REASONS FACE-TO-FACE WITH GOD?

YES   NO

NOW, LET'S THINK ABOUT THOSE THINGS YOU HAVE TO BE THANKFUL FOR...

1. _____
2. _____
3. _____
4. _____
5. _____

REMEMBER: PRAYER CHANGES THINGS!!!

WE LEARNED OBEDIENCE THROUGH THE THINGS WE SUFFERED

1. _____
2. _____
3. _____
4. _____
5. _____

HEBREWS 5:8 KJV

THOUGH HE WERE A SON, YET LEARNED HE OBEDIENCE BY THE THINGS WHICH HE SUFFERED

I NEED TO REMEMBER

1. _____
2. _____
3. _____
4. _____
5. _____

NOTES:

RECITE THESE:

When did God say that while we are here on earth, we will not hurt?
We will
We will have trials and tribulations for "Him" to see us through
Step aside and see what God will do
Christians, it's these things that keep us humbled
Oh, we may stumble
But don't give up
Don't give in
Pick yourself up and start again

Start reciting the following:
I have faith
I am holding on
I am strong
I do believe
I do trust Him
For God never fails

DEEP STATEMENTS

JUST SAY NO

I SHALL LIVE, I SHALL NOT DIE

I'M NOT THE SAVIOR

HE KNOWS MY NAME

I NEED THEE EVERY HOUR

NOT MY TIMING, BUT HIS

CAST ALL MY CARES UPON HIM
FOR HE CARETH FOR ME

AND MORE...

_____

_____

_____

_____

PRAY WITHOUT CEASING

Lord, thank You for being You! I appreciate You and want to be a godly example and blessing. Lord, forgive my sins! I love You! You are a mighty God! Awesome God! I thank You for Your grace, mercy, and unmerited favor! I am so happy You have the last say. Thank You for providing for me, my family, and friends! Thank You that no weapon formed against me shall prosper! Hallelujah! I speak life. I shall live and I shall not die! Thank You for the plan You have for my life! My desire is to be pleasing in Your sight in the matchless name of Jesus!

Amen.

GOD'S PROMISES

JESUS WILL HELP ME IF I'M TEMPTED.

HEBREWS 2:18

IF I RESIST THE DEVIL, HE WILL FLEA.

JAMES 4:7

IF I DRAW NEAR TO GOD, HE WILL DRAW NEAR TO ME.

JAMES 4:8

IF I ASK, HE WILL PROVIDE.

JAMES 4:2

HE FORGIVES AND CLEANSES ME AS I CONFESS MY SINS TO HIM.

1 JOHN 1:9

GOD WILL KEEP ME IN PERFECT PEACE IF MY MIND IS STAYED ON HIM.

ISAIAH 26:3

HE CARES FOR ME.

1 PETER 5:7O

ALL THINGS WORK TOGETHER FOR MY GOOD.

ROMANS 8:2:58

GOD WON'T LET ME BE TRIED OR TEMPTED BEYOND WHAT I CAN HANDLE.

           1 CORINTIANS 10:13

I WILL REAP WHAT I SOW.

           GALATIANS 6:7

GOD WILL SUPPLY ALL MY NEEDS.

           PHILIPPIANS 4:19

GOD HAS GIVEN ME ETERNAL LIFE.

           1 JOHN 5-11

PRAYER IS EFFECTIVE.

           JAMES 5:16

STANDING ON THE PROMISES

What's stressing you?

Go into your closet and shout it out!

Breathe…

Then learn a promise of God that relates to your stressor and recite it throughout the day.

Encourage yourself in the Lord!

Now, watch how strong you become…

Standing on the Promises of God!!!

Hallelujah!!!

Thank you, Lord!!!

MY DESIRE IS.........
TO BE PLEASING IN GOD'S SIGHT.

YOUR DESIRE(S).........

_____

_____

_____

_____

_____

_____

_____

_____

_____

_____

_____

_____

BIBLE VERSES FOR SOME OF YOUR SITUATIONS

PEOPLE FAIL YOU	PSALM 27
SINNED	PSALM 51
WORRY	MATT 6:19-34
DANGER	PSALM 91
SORROW	JOHN 14
FEARFUL	PSALM 23
DOWN AND OUT	ROMANS 8:39
DISCOURAGED	ISAIAH 40
GOD SEEMS DISTANT	PSALM 139
NEED COURAGE	JOSHUA 1
BLUES	PSALM 34
WHEN THE DEVIL SEEMS BIGGER	PSALM 90
TRAVELING	PSALM 121/107
BITTER	1 CORINTHIANS 1
INVESTMENTS	MARK 10:17-31

IF YOU NEED AN ENCOURAGING WORD... EMAIL ME AT:

cwilliamswarren@gmail.com

IN NEED OF PRAYER AND/OR A CHURCH HOME? CONSIDER:

NEW BEGINNINGS APOSTOLIC FAITH MINISTRIES
ELDER MARY KING, PASTOR
1001 WEST RD
CHESAPEAKE, VA 23323
757-337-0098

BISHOP JOSEPH KING & PASTOR MARY L. KING
WWW.NewbeginningsApostolicfaithministries.com
NBAFM RADIO MINISTRY
WPCE 1400
WEDNESDAY'S @11:45

New Calvary Baptist Church
Rev. Dr. WM Marcus Small, Senior Pastor
800 E. Virginia Beach Blvd
Norfolk, VA 23504
757-627-1269

Living Destiny Church
Pastor Moses
6204 N. Military Hwy
Norfolk, VA 23518
757-321-7486

CANICE "MRS. REALTY" LASSITER

COVERED QWEEN

FOR YOUR REALITY NEEDS

757-986-9800

canice@mrs-reality.com

SPECIALITY T- SHIRTS AND MORE.....

JUST ASK

ALSO.....

GEORGE LASSITER

FOR Y0UR LAWNCARE AND/OR HAULING NEEDS

#powermovebro

AND MORE...

SINCE READING THIS BOOK, WHAT HAS CHANGED?

_____
_____
_____
_____
_____
_____
_____
_____
_____
_____
_____
_____
_____
_____
_____
_____

WORD FIND

```
A C P E B X U F D S S R O N O E E E E I T R O M M S J
G Q M B V A A G D V D V S E R R P S I O C C Y J X K L
A G T S L O F R W C O N M V I C T O R Y J J B X V N O
B T S T A W L A N X M W X A W V T P U R E W O P Z A I
F M G F E H F C C P E A C E S I Y R O Q C R Z R Q H S
V Y I L H O M E L T R U T H R N X U W B Q E P O H T T
P A F N L T N N F S C K W X C C E P P V E V U T R M P
M A T A D D F F H L Y T I N I R T Z Z U C L F E X O W
N U S K V H F F O C P L L S O A E A U Q G S C C Z D A
L P V I S O O W G E P W W P A A R S B G X A L T N S S
C V W J B J R E C N A T I R E H N I R J E L B I B I L
Z Q E B I V G J R L R K L J C A I O E P N V H O L W A
V I P R O M I S E S E E Y Y D A T E L Q H A B N E P O
Z G R E J K V O R O N R I X G B Y U A F Q T X J S G N
D D A N C E E Y V C T B S A U B O E T S H I J C S R A
I W I E V W N O I I S X F A I T H N I L L O R H I R B
X Q S G O W E J A A Q I U E D O N X O Z F N E F N E W
P A E U W Q S X A A S A L V A T I O N G H D F J G Y U
G R S J L K S N N N G Z S O N G G H S J Y W I D S A U
S X J W I L L Q R R D J V T C W Z B H S A Z U X U R R
P K M P F A I T X X Y D A O E H C D I X Q J E O H P C
Z L Q N E O T V W D I R E C T I O N P B V H P A J Z Z
```

LOVE	TRINITY	FOREGIVENESS	GUIDANCE
PARENTS	GRACE	GIFTS	PRAISE
MERCY	HEAVEN	HOPE	HEAL
PEACE	POWER	FAITH	DELIVERER
ETERNITY	BLESSINGS	PROTECTION	JUDGE
TRUTH	BIBLE	VICTORY	SONG
DIRECTION	SALVATION	RELATIONSHIP	DANCE
FAVOR	JOY	THANKS	HOME
LIFE	PROMISES	WISDOM	PRAYER
WILL	PURPOSE	INHERITENCE	MIND

HOW MANY WORDS CAN YOU MAKE OUT OF THESE LETTERS?:

R A E P

O S U G

D I L W

NOTES:

7

THE NUMBER OF COMPLETION.

I REST.

NEXT>>>>>>>>>>>>>>>>>>>>>>>>>>

Connie Williams Warren lives in Norfolk, Virginia but is originally from Virginia Beach, Virginia.

"Misspoetress" started writing poetry and encouraging words as a young child. Now at 62-years-young, she has finally decided to publish one of her books, proving as C. S. Lewis said, that "you are never too old to set another goal or dream a new dream." To God be the glory!!!

This workbook will give hope to people who are thinking that no one understands and no one cares, and it is focused on letting you know that you are not alone! You too can accomplish your goals with the help of God reminding you that everyone has things to be thankful about. Connie's book helps you to look in the mirror and participate in a sort of workbook style while having some fun doing so! Read, share, and enjoy my book "BUT GOD BY GOD".

www.ingramcontent.com/pod-product-compliance
Lightning Source LLC
LaVergne TN
LVHW051510070426
835507LV00022B/3035